Chase the Moon, Tiny Turtle

A Hatchling's Daring Race to the Sea

For Mom, who loves turtles and the seashore.
— K. J.

For my world: Adam, Sadie, & Elliott.
— S. W.

Text copyright © 2021 Kelly Jordan
Illustrations copyright © 2021 Sally Walker

First published in 2021 by Page Street Kids
an imprint of
Page Street Publishing Co.
27 Congress Street, Suite 1511
Salem, MA 01970
www.pagestreetpublishing.com

Distributed by Macmillan, sales in Canada by The Canadian Manda Group

24 25 26 CCO 7 6

ISBN-13: 978-1-64567-152-7. ISBN-10: 1-64567-152-6

CIP data for this book is available from the Library of Congress.

This book was typeset in Farewell Angelina. The illustrations were done using printmaking, digital,
and traditional materials. Cover and book design by Melia Parsloe for Page Street Kids.

Printed and bound in Shenzhen, Guangdong, China

Page Street Publishing uses only materials from suppliers who are committed to responsible and
sustainable forest management.

Page Street Publishing protects our planet by donating to nonprofits like The Trustees,
which focuses on local land conservation.

Chase the Moon, Tiny Turtle

A Hatchling's Daring Race to the Sea

Kelly Jordan

illustrated by Sally Walker

PAGE STREET KIDS

Up, bright! Silver light,
little egg, summer night.

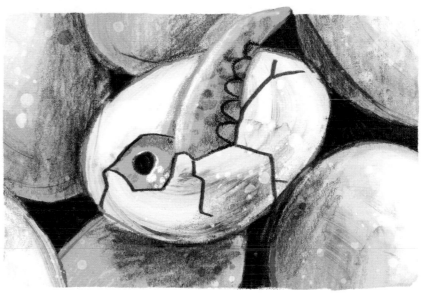

Tap-a-tap. Push, *creak*.
Crack the shell. Sneak a peek.

Dig! Heave! Sisters, brothers.
Break ground. Join the others.

Head tipped back, take it in.
Feel cool air on your skin.

Rolling waves, diamond skies.
Lunar path, brand-new eyes.

Soft beams coax, "Chase the moon."
Walk to water. Home soon.

Crunch. Whistle. Hooting owls.

Shriek, splash, whoosh! Piercing howls.

Swipe, swipe.

Left then right.

Tiny turtle, hungry night.

Duck! Scuttle. Shiver. Go!
Chase the moon's gentle glow.

Keep on course. Watch the tracks.
Journey close with the pack.

Rushing wind, swaying trees.
Salty air, crashing seas.

Press forward. Chase the moon.
Use your instincts. Home soon.

Snip-snap. Clicking claws.

Quick! Faster! Dodge those paws!

Catch the wave. Use your shell.
Surf, turtle. Ride the swell!

Midnight swimmer,
glide until . . .

all is quiet. All is still.

Dive down deep.

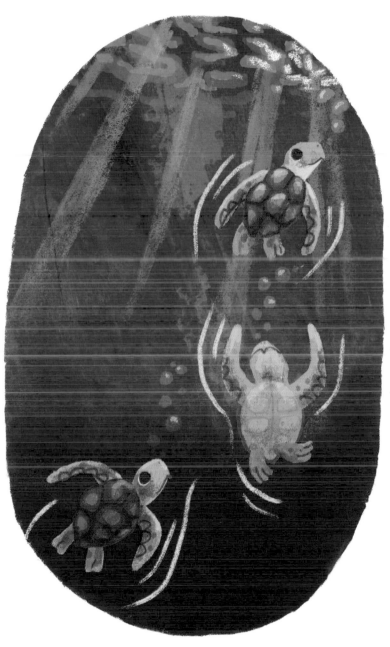

Home soon.

Open ocean.
Chase the moon.

From Nest to Sea:
A Hatchling's Journey

Female loggerhead turtles travel thousands of miles to lay about one hundred eggs in a "clutch" on the same beach where they were born. When it's time, the turtle hatchlings break from their shells using a spike on their beak called a "caruncle," or "egg tooth." Then they push through the sand and start the dangerous journey to the ocean, following the light reflected from the moon. Along the way, they encounter land predators such as ghost crabs, shorebirds, raccoons, feral hogs, dogs, and fire ants. But the hatchlings' journey doesn't end once they arrive at the water; they continue to swim to the open sea, where they live near large patches of seaweed for several years as they grow.

Be a Hatchling Helper!

- **Watch your waste.** Turtles often ingest, become tangled in, or choke on plastic items. Instead of throwing plastic in the trash after a single use, recycle or reuse it instead.

- **Turn off the lights.** Since sea turtles rely on the moon's reflection to lead them to the ocean, it's important to turn off any lights near nesting sites so hatchlings don't head in the wrong direction—and into harm's way.

- **Champion the sea turtles.** If you live by the coast or an area where sea turtles nest, ask your local nature center if there are opportunities for you to volunteer with a turtle patrol or a turtle count. Share your sea turtle knowledge with your friends, family, and classmates and teach others how they can help too!